Numerical investigation of helium bubble rising behavior in cross-type channel

Chunjie Zeng
Zhaoming Meng

ELIVA PRESS

Chunjie Zeng

Zhaoming Meng

In a certain nuclear reactor, the coolant channel is a cross-type channel, there is little research about bubble rising behavior in this kind of channel, but the neutron detection would be affected by the bubbles. Through comparing with previous experiment, proper numerical model has been determined, then studied the cross-type channel under different helium flow rates with CFD software Fluent. Research shows that the bubble distribution exists some similarities under different helium flow rates, the bubbles tend to rise near the tube wall; In the axial direction of the flow channel, the bubble coalescence can be observed, which leads the section void fraction in the axial direction to increase first and then tends to be stable, and the section void fraction increases with increasing helium flow rates.

Published: Eliva Press SRL
Address: MD-2060, bd.Cuza-Voda, 1/4, of. 21 Chişinău, Republica
Moldova
Email: info@elivapress.com
Website: www.elivapress.com

ISBN: 978-1-952751-50-9

© Eliva Press SRL
© Chunjie Zeng, Zhaoming Meng
Cover Design: Eliva Press SRL

Numerical investigation of helium bubble rising behavior in cross-type channel

Chunjie Zeng[1,2], Baoxin Yuan[3], Zhaoming Meng[1]*, Xin Zhang[4], Herui Jiang[1], Defang Mu[2], Ruihao Yan[1]

(*[1]College of Nuclear Science and Technology, Harbin Engineering University, Harbin, 150001, China, [2]School of Nuclear Science and Technology, Xi'an Jiaotong University, Xi'an, 710049, China, [3]China Academy of Engineering Physics, Sichuan, 621900, China, [4]Institute of Nuclear and New Energy Technology, Tsinghua University, Beijing, 100084, China)*

Abstract :

In a certain nuclear reactor, the coolant channel is a cross-type channel. There is little research about bubble rising behavior in this kind of channel, but the neutron detection would be affected by the bubbles. Through comparing with previous experiment, proper numerical model has been determined, and the cross-type channel under different helium flow rates is studied with CFD software Fluent. Research shows that the bubble distribution exhibits some similarities under different helium flow rates, and the bubbles tend to rise near the tube wall; In the axial direction of the flow channel, the bubble coalescence can be observed, which leads the void fraction in the axial direction to increase first and then to be stable; The void fraction increases with increasing helium flow rates.

Keywords: CFD; Fluent; Bubble; Cross-type channel; Void fraction

Zeng C, Yuan B, Meng Z, Zhang X, Jiang H, Mu D and Yan R (2020) Numerical Investigation of Helium Bubble Rising Behavior in Cross-Type Channel. Front. Energy Res. 8:184. doi: 10.3389/fenrg.2020.00184

Content

1. Introduction

The cross-section of the coolant channel is cross-shape in a certain nuclear reactor, and in some cases there are hydrogen bubbles in it. Under the effect of various forces such as buoyancy, resistance, pressure, etc., the bubbles are unstable (the trajectory of the rising bubbles is not a line, but more like the "Z", and also the shape of bubbles changes a lot) during the rising process, which leads to significant deformation and coalescence. The existence of these bubbles in the channel will cause errors in neutron detection in the nuclear reactor, furthermore it will affect the safety of the reactor. so it is of great necessity to do some research about the bubble rising behavior in cross-type channel, which can help other researchers know where to put the neutron detector is better (less influence by bubbles).

There are two types of research about submerged bubbles rising: submerged jet upward and submerged jet downward as shown in Fig. 1. These researches are mainly carried out in a large water tank or conventional pipe, through submerging a small diameter pipe with gas to generate bubbles to study the laws of bubble formation, detachment, rising behavior etc. In the submerged jet upward, the effects of surface tension, nozzle diameter, gas flow rates, liquid density, liquid viscosity, rolling conditions etc. have been extensively studied[1][2][3][4][5][6]. There exists bubble coalescence during the rising process of multiple bubbles. Related researches have been performed by Yu Haijing[3] and Huang Ying[7]; In the submerged jet downward, the influencing factors of bubble formation and detachment are also related to the immersion depth of the nozzle, nozzle shape, the inner and outer diameter etc.[8][9][10][11]. In these researches, the focus is on the study of bubbles formation and detachment, but less attention is paid to the distribution of bubbles during the rising process. On the other hand, considering the effect of wall on the rising bubbles, the study about rising bubble in a narrow rectangular channel has been carried out[12][13]. However, these studies about narrow rectangular channel also can't reflect the situation in the cross-type flow channel. The width of the cross-type flow channel is wider than a narrow rectangular one, and the cross-type flow channel is not a conventional channel which causes bubble motion more complex. On the other hand, the previous researches did not pay much attention to the void fraction in the axial direction of the flow channel, but void fraction can exactly reflect the influence of the bubbles on neutron detection in the reactor. In summary, existing researches, neither bubble rising behavior in large-sized flow channels nor narrow rectangular channels can well reflect the situation in cross-type flow channel.

The most advantage of numerical simulation is cheap, and it can get more detailed parameters than experiments. So the purpose of the present study is to investigate the rising behavior of helium bubbles (considering that the helium is often used instead of hydrogen for research in the laboratory) in cross-type channel through CFD numerical simulations, which can provide a basis for the improvement of neutron detector in the nuclear reactor.

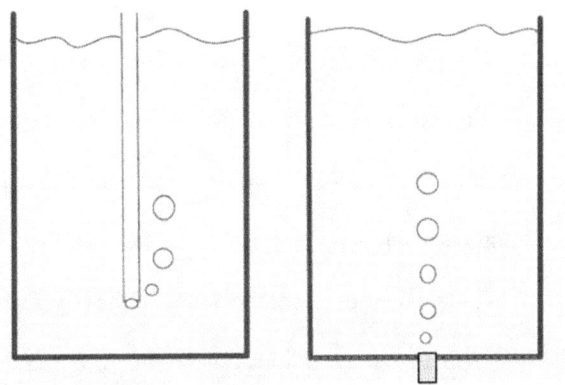

Fig. 1. Submerged jet downward (left) & Submerged jet upward (right)

2. Numerical simulations

2.1 Numerical model

The VOF model[14] is built on the premise that two or more fluids (or phases) do not mix with each other, which is used to track the moving interface. The basic principle is to use the volume fraction of each phase in each grid cell and the corresponding function to determine the interface of each phase, so as to indirectly determine the changes of the fluids, rather than track the movement of the particles on the interface. When dealing with the volume fraction of different phases passing through the region, the VOF model assumes that there is a clear interface between the different phases, and there is no interpenetration between each other. This makes the volume fraction of each phase independent of each other, which means when a phase is added, a corresponding volume fraction equation is introduced, combining with each corresponding separate momentum equation, the simulation of the motion of two or more fluids can be realized. In each control unit, the sum of the volume fractions of all phases is 1. When calculating each unit, the properties and volume fractions of each phase are used to obtain a volume average value of the physical parameters in the unit. The obtained average value is shared by every phase in the unit, so that the properties in the grid unit may be a certain phase or a mixture of multiple phases, which depending on the volume fraction. In other words, in the unit, if the volume fraction of the nth phase fluid is α_n, there are 3 kinds of situations:

a）$\alpha_n=0$：There is no nth phase in the unit;

b）$\alpha_n=1$：Filled with nth phase in the unit;

c）$0<\alpha_n<1$：There exists interface between nth phase and another phase (or other phases).

The SST (shear stress transport) k-ω model[Error! Reference source not found.] was developed from the Baseline k-ω model. The SST k-ω model combined the stability of standard k-ω model near the wall and the independence of the k-ε model outside the boundary layer. Also the propagation of turbulent shear stress affected by the turbulent viscosity was considered. The SST k-ω model has higher accuracy and credibility in the simulation of various complex flow conditions than the standard k-ω and k-ε model.

2.2 Validation

For researching the law of bubble formation in the process of gas-liquid stirring during the industrial production, an experiment of submerged jet directed upward has been done by Lu Wei[9], as shown in Fig. 2. And the data like bubble size under several flow rates has been achieved.

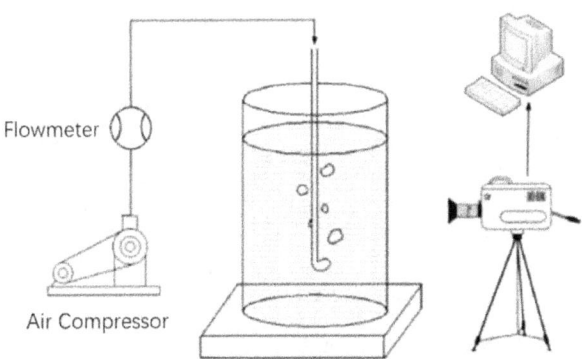

Flowmeter

Air Compressor

Fig. 2. Schematic diagram of experimental apparatus[9]

In this experiment, the bubble that has just left the nozzle is selected as the research object, at this time, the bottom of the bubble just rises to be aligned with the bottom end of the nozzle. In the horizontal direction, the size of the bubble is obtained directly by the ruler; in the vertical direction, the distance between the top and bottom of the bubble is measured, which is the vertical size of the bubble. Fig. 3 shows the selection criteria.

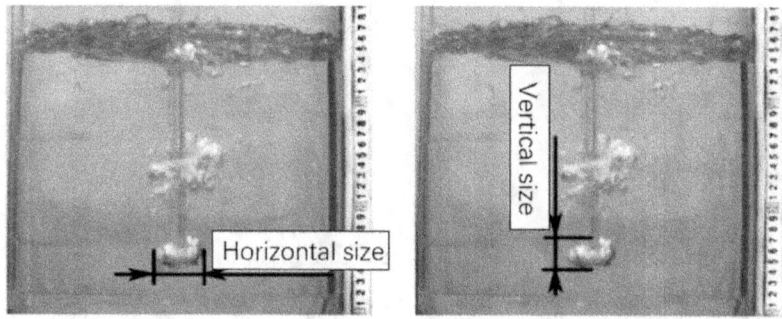

Fig. 3. Selection criteria of bubble size[9]

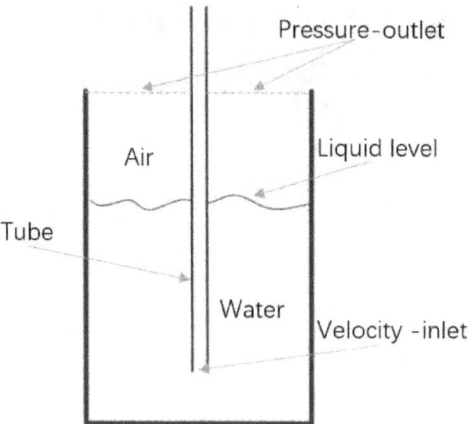

Fig. 4. Schematic diagram of numerical simulation

In order to validate the rationality of the adopted numerical method, a corresponding numerical simulation model according to Lu Wei[9]'s experiment has been established. Fig. 4 shows the schematic diagram.

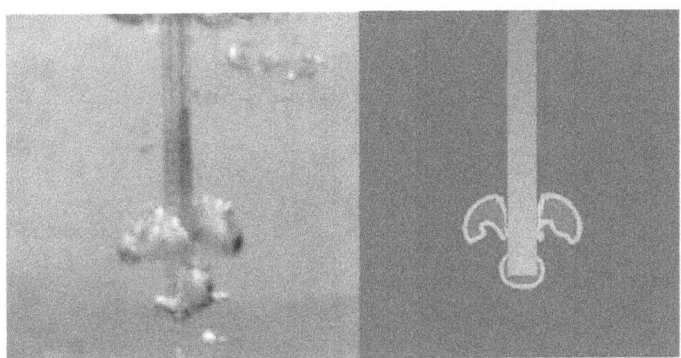

Fig. 5. The comparison of Lu Wei[9]'s experiment results and simulation results

The similarity in Fig. 5 preliminarily illustrates the rationality of the simulation method. Furthermore, the bubble size of experimental results and numerical results have been compared as shown in Fig. 6. The maximum error between the numerical results and the experimental results does not exceed 12.2%, and the trend of the increase of the bubble size with the increase of the helium rates is also coincident. Considering that the numerical simulation itself is under the ideal conditions, so the error is acceptable, which verifies the correctness of this numerical method.

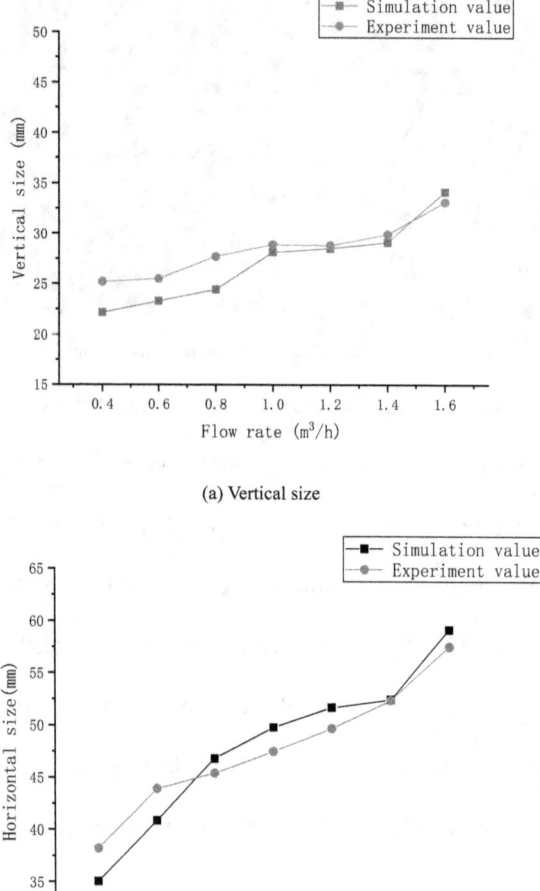

(a) Vertical size

(b) Horizontal size

Fig. 6. Bubble size comparison

2.3 Simulation of cross-type channel

Fig. 7 shows the cross-type channel model, the axial length of the channel is 185.25l, the outer diameter of the tube is 1.33l (the inner diameter is l, l=6.1mm) in size, and the tube reaches 3.28l from the bottom of the flow channel. Fig. 7 also shows the radial size of flow channel.

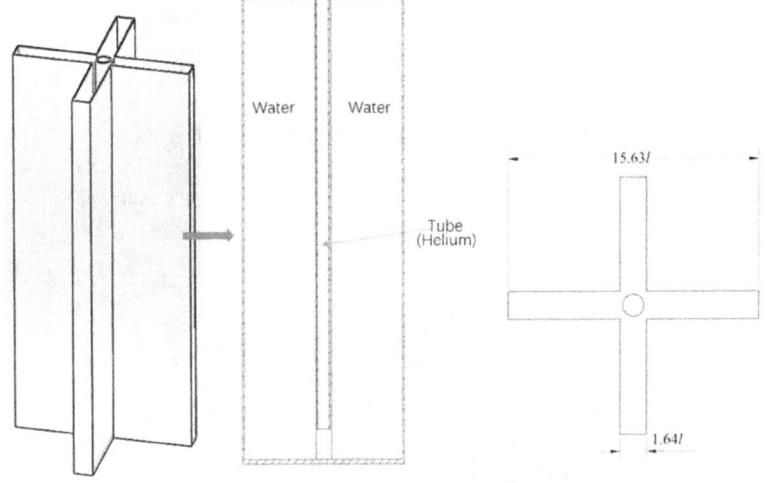

Fig. 7. Cross-type channel model and radial size

Considering that the cross-type channel is a symmetric structure, a quarter symmetry is adopted to improve the calculation efficiency. The calculation domain is shown in of Fig. 8 (the region inside the red frame), and there are two symmetric boundaries, the velocity inlet is used at the bottom of the pipe. The top of the cross-type channel is the pressure outlet, and the rest are the walls. We used hexahedral grids, and the wall surface and the inlet part are densified. Because it is a transient problem, the PISO algorithm is adopted. For the convergence condition, the Fluent default values are used.

Aiming to the number of cells of 481181, 845306 and 1622105, the validation of mesh independence has been established. Four different inlet helium flow rates from 0.06 to 1.2m/s were selected as the comparison conditions under different number of cells. As shown in Fig. 9, the bubble sizes (the bubbles measured at the exit of the nozzle as described above) are almost the same (order of 0.1mm) with these under the number of cells of 845306 and 1622105, even the gap between 481181 grids and 1622105 grids is small. So in this research a meshing method between 481181 and 845306 grids is adopted.

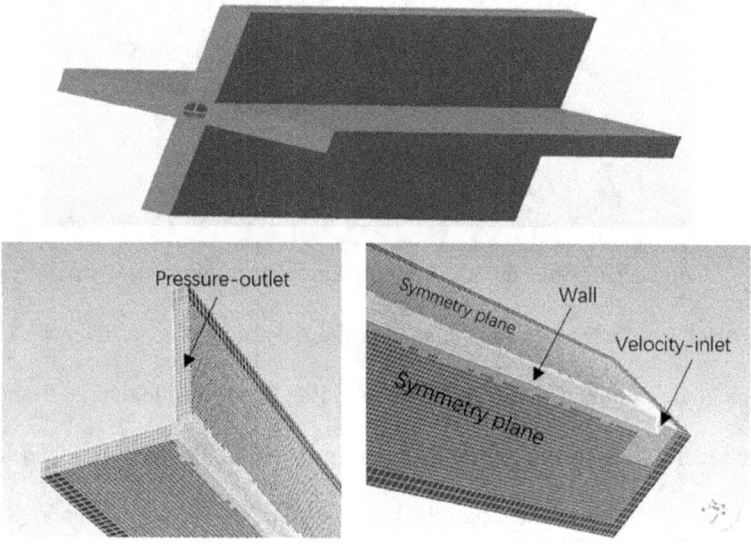

Fig. 8 Computational domain, mesh and boundary conditions

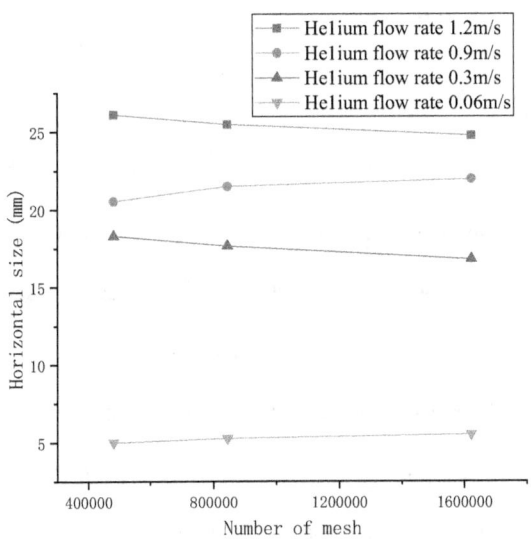

(a) Horizontal size

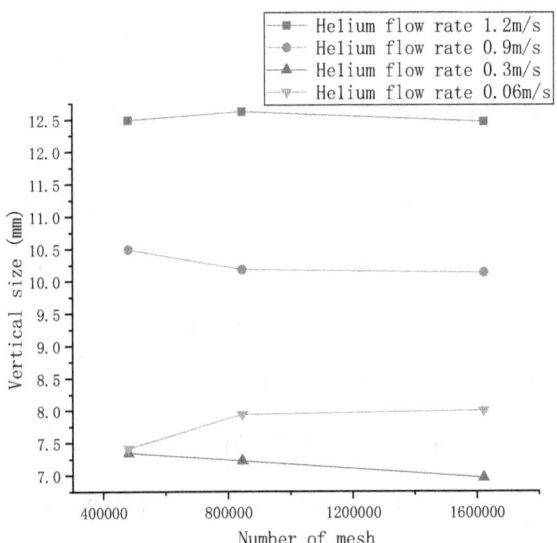

(b) Vertical size

Fig. 9. Bubble size comparison

3. Results and discussion

In this study, a numerical simulation of helium flow rates from 0.01L/min to 2L/min was carried out. The study found that some characteristics of bubbles have obvious regularity under different flow rates of helium. Due to space limitations, the following will select some representative working conditions for detailed discussion.

For the sake of analysis, the channel has been divided into three parts, the inlet is z=0m, the region of z <0.2m is called bottom area, 0.2m <z <0.6m is middle area, z > 0.6m is top area as shown in Fig. 10.

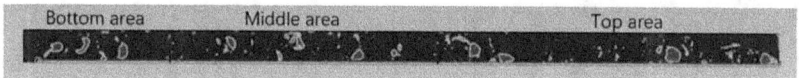

Fig. 10. Flow channel division

3.1 Research on bubble distribution characteristics

Through the contours of phases and animation in the axial direction of the cross-type channel, we found that the bubble size increased with the increase of helium flow rates, manifesting the area occupied by the helium (red one) became larger and larger in the axial section, as shown in Fig. 11; Combining the animation of the contours of phases in the axial and radial sections, it can be seen that most bubbles tended to rise near the tube wall (the smaller the flow rates are, the more obvious it will be). There were also a few smaller bubbles distributed far away from the tube wall (some can reach one of the four corners of the cross-type channel), and move downward during the process of bubble rising.

In the radial section, take the helium flow rate of 2L/min for instance. As shown in Fig. 12, at z = 0m, the distribution of helium was concentrated at the nozzle. Initially, the shape of the bubble was relatively regular, and the helium distribution at the cross-section was approximately circular (quarter symmetry), but then the bubble gradually became irregular, as shown in Fig. 12 (a) t=3.040s, the helium distribution on the cross-section was biased to one side. The reason is that the rising bubbles detached from the nozzle cause the flow disturbance which makes the bubbles near nozzle under complex stress. Fig. 13 shows the radial helium distribution at helium flow rate of 0.5L/min. It is similar to other working conditions, just the proportion of helium in the cross-section of the flow channel decreasing with reduction of helium flow rates.

Overall, at high flow rates (above 1L/min), the movement of bubbles in the flow channel is similar to the slug flow in a vertical pipe. At low flow rates (below 0.1L/min), the form is similar to the bubbly flow in a vertical pipe.

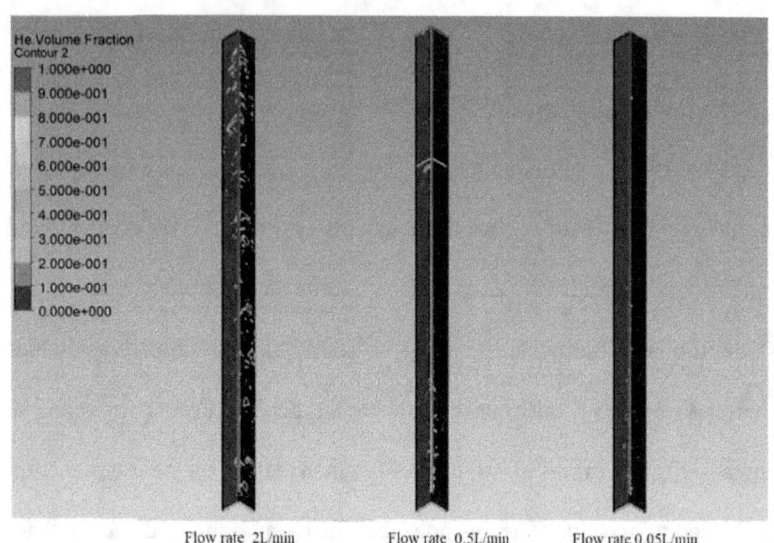

Flow rate 2L/min   Flow rate 0.5L/min   Flow rate 0.05L/min

Fig. 11. Axial helium distribution under different flow rates

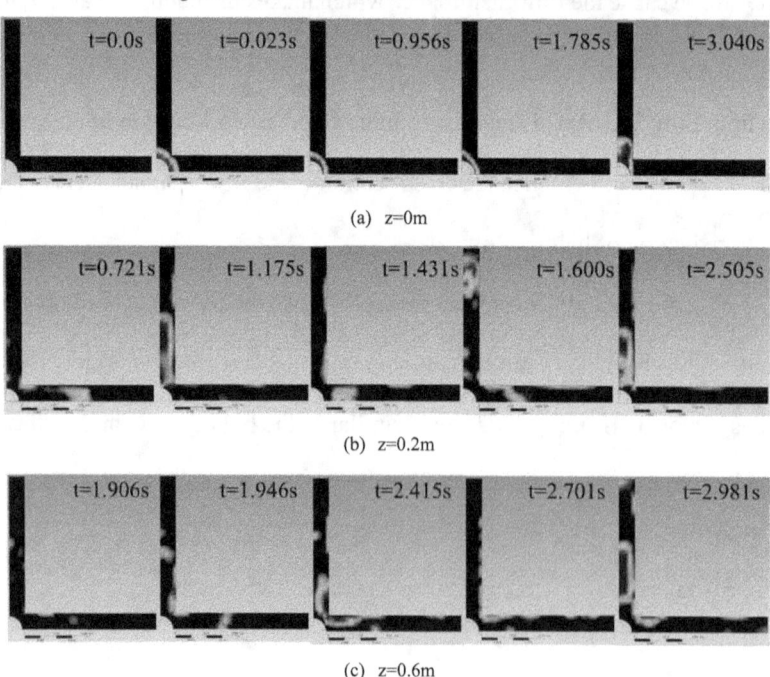

(a) z=0m

(b) z=0.2m

(c) z=0.6m

Fig. 12. Contours of helium distribution for helium flow rates is 2L/min

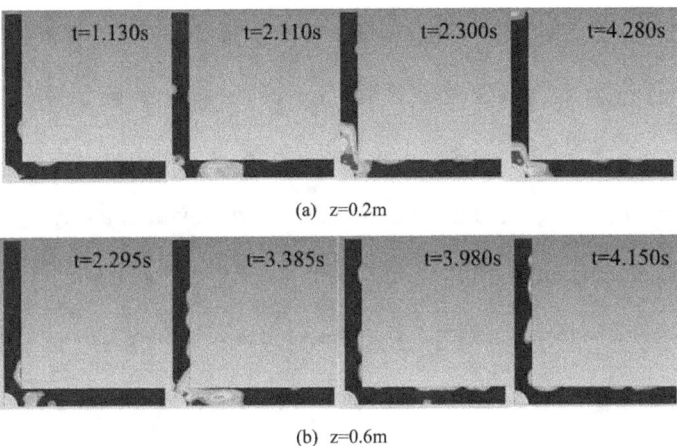

(a) z=0.2m

(b) z=0.6m

Fig. 13. Contours of helium distribution for helium flow rates is 0.5L/min

3.2 Research on the characteristics of bubble coalescence

Through flow animation under different flow rates, it can be found that in the middle area and top area of the flow channel, large bubbles were distributed at a certain interval in the axial direction, and among the large bubbles were small bubbles (not obvious when helium flow rates is lower than 0.1L/min) as shown in Fig. 14.

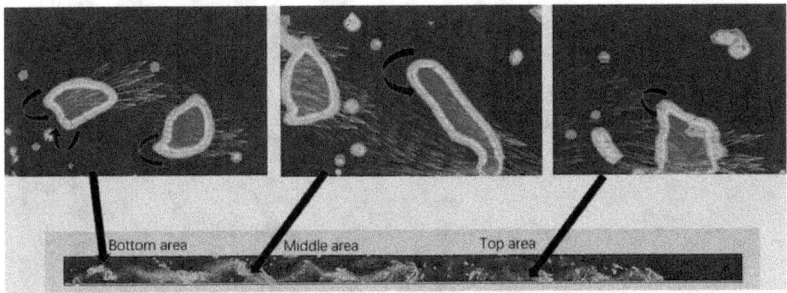

Fig. 14. Velocity vector distribution in the flow channel for helium flow rates is 2L/min

During the process of bubble rising, the motion of fluid around the bubble will affect the subsequent bubbles. Taking the velocity vector distribution at the flow rate of 2L/min for instance as shown in Fig. 14, the direction of the fluid vector on the side of the rising bubble was opposite. This is why some small bubbles move downward within a certain range. Also, the direction of the fluid vector at the tail of the rising bubble was the same, which accelerated the subsequent bubbles to catch up with the previous one, then bubble coalescence happened. In the axial direction, the bubbles were getting larger and larger due to the bubble coalescence, which leads to an upward trend in void fraction at the bottom area of the flow channel along the axial direction. In the area after the middle area of flow channel, as the bubbles were accelerated by buoyancy, the distance among bubbles became large, which weakened the influence of surrounding fluid on bubbles. Finally, large bubbles were distributed at a certain interval, and some small bubbles were separated among the large bubbles.

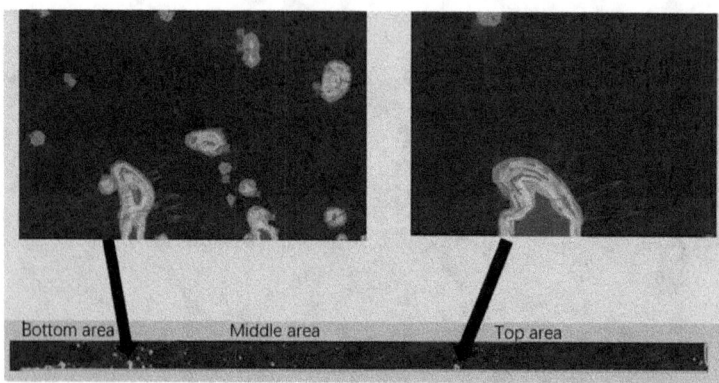

Fig. 15. Velocity vector distribution in the flow channel for helium flow rates is 0.5L/min

Fig. 15 shows the velocity vector distribution of helium flow rates 0.5L/min. Compared with the condition of 2L/min, the rising bubbles had less disturbance on the flow field, but the bubble coalescence still exited, especially at the bottom area of the channel. It was just not as frequent as the helium flow rates of 2L/min. Fig. 16 shows the condition of helium flow rates 0.50L/min. As the flow rates of helium gas was further decreased, the bubble volume became smaller and smaller, and the flow channel space occupied also became smaller, so that the disturbance caused by the rising bubble became smaller, as a result, the frequency of the bubble coalescence is reduced.

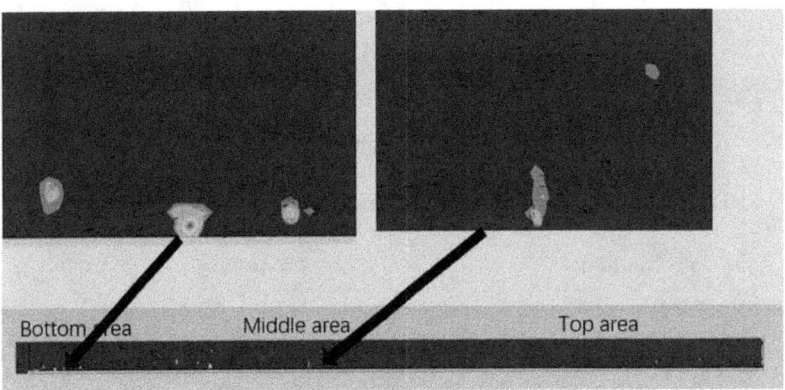

Fig. 16. Velocity vector distribution in the flow channel for helium flow rates is 0.05L/min

3.3 Research on the influence of flow rate on the void fraction

Analyzing 10 planes in the axial direction of the flow channel, they are planes of z=0, z=0.02, z=0.04, z=0.06, z=0.08, z=0.1, z=0.2, z=0.4, z=0.6, z=0.8m respectively, as shown in Fig. 17.

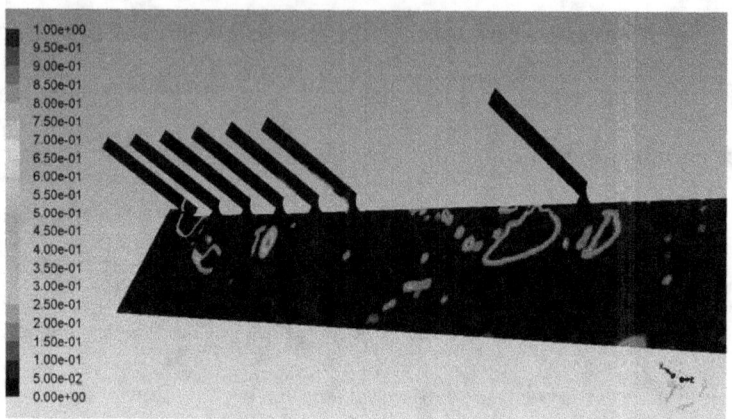

Fig. 17. Part of selected planes

The void fraction of a plane can be obtained through calculating the proportion of the helium share in the selected plane. The graph of the void fraction of each plane with time is shown as followed (The green dotted line is the average of the void fraction).

(b) The average of the void fraction

Fig. 18 shows the curve of void fraction versus time and the average of the void fraction.

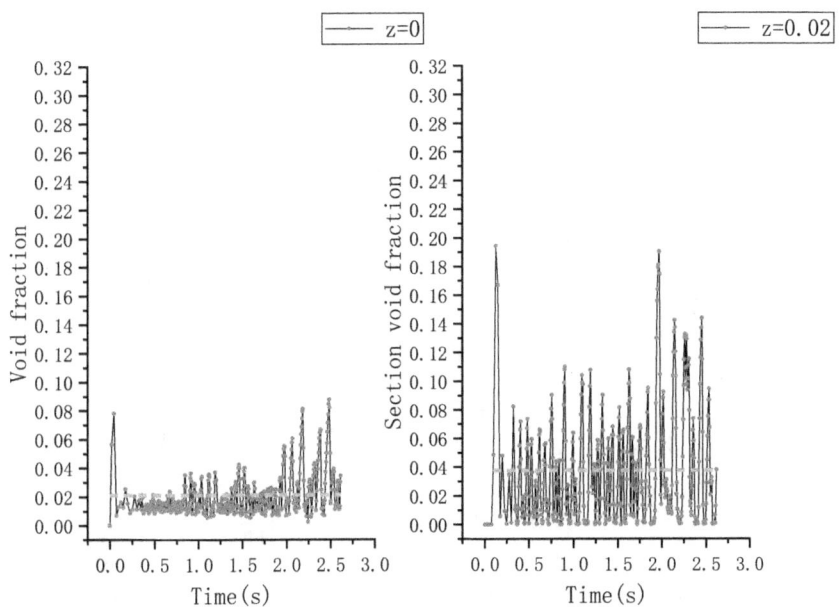

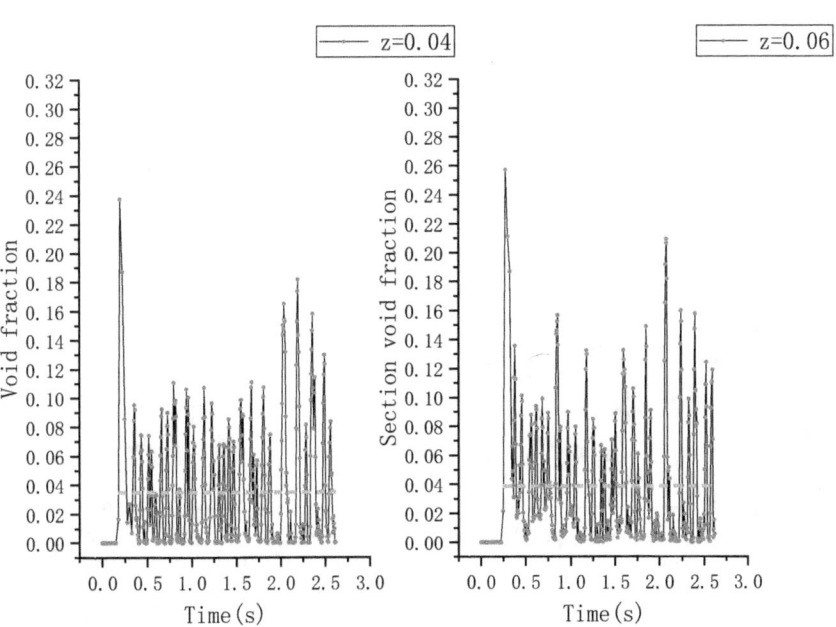

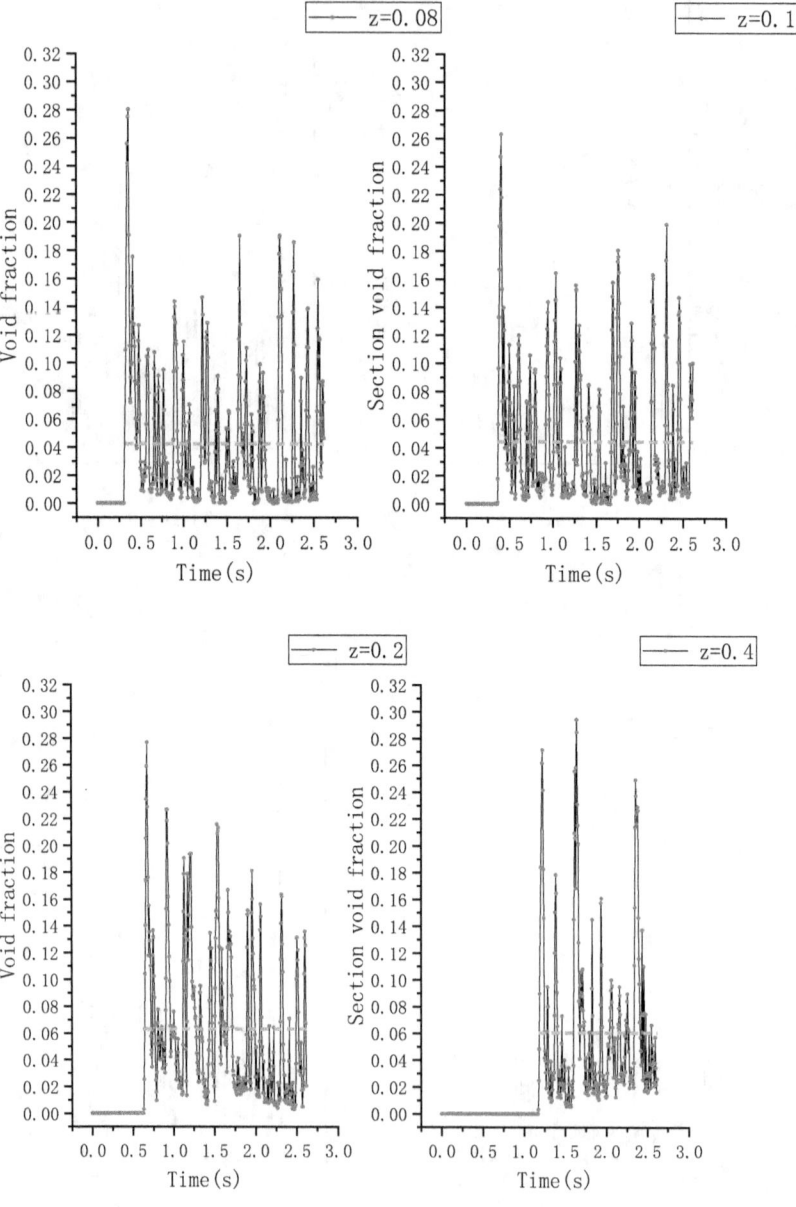

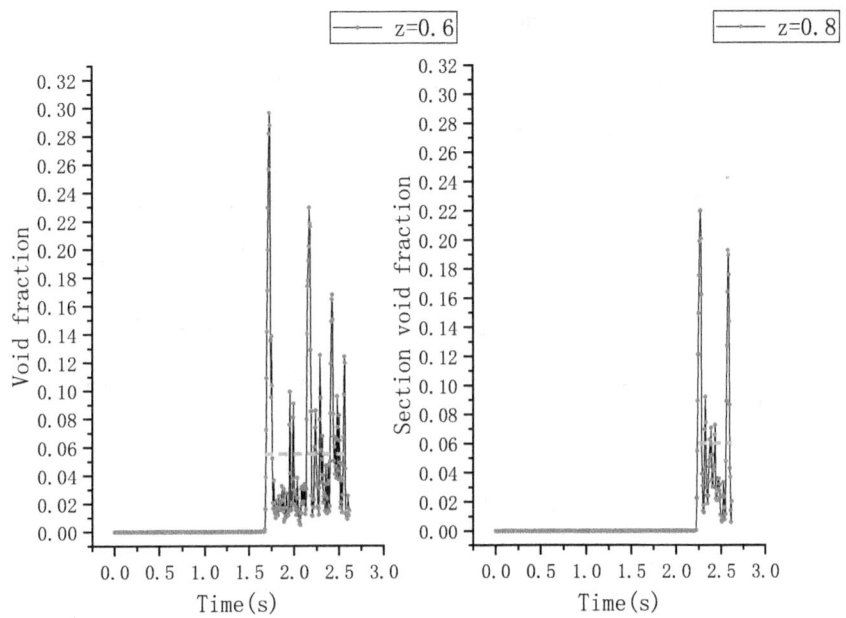

(a) The void fraction versus time and different planes

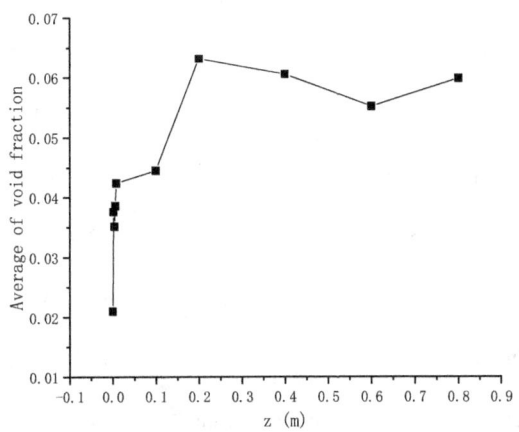

(b) The average of the void fraction

Fig. 18. Curve of void fraction, 2L/min helium flow rates

The figures above show that, during a period of time, the larger value of the transient void fraction occurs less frequently (the maximum transient void fraction can reach 0.3), which leads to a lower average void fraction (the maximum average void fraction can only reach 0.063); In the bottom area of the flow channel, the average value of the void fraction increases rapidly with increasing axial position. In the middle area and the top area of the flow channel, the average value of the void fraction does not change much.

The reason for the above phenomenon is the bubble coalescence, as analyzed in Section 3.2. Within a certain distance, the latter bubble is accelerated by the disturbance of flow field and will catch up with the previous bubble, which leads to bubble coalescence. As a result, causing an upward trend in void fraction of the bottom area of the flow channel in the axial direction, and in the middle area and top area of the flow channel, due to the accelerated rising bubbles by the buoyancy, the distance among bubbles in the axial direction becomes larger, resulting in the decrease of bubble coalescence frequency. Eventually, large bubbles are distributed at a certain interval, and some small bubbles are separated by large bubbles, this is why the maximum value of the void fraction of a certain cross-section is much larger than the average value.

When the flow rates of helium are 0.5L/min, the variation law of the void fraction in the axial direction of the flow channel is similar to the situation of 2L/min helium flow rates: the maximum transient void fraction of a plane of the flow channel is much larger than its average value. (maximum transient void fraction can reach 0.14, and maximum average void fraction is only 0.019); in the bottom area of the flow channel, the average void fraction increases rapidly, while in the middle area and top area of the flow channel does not change much and tends to be stable. Fig. 19 shows the curve of void fraction versus time and the average of the void fraction.

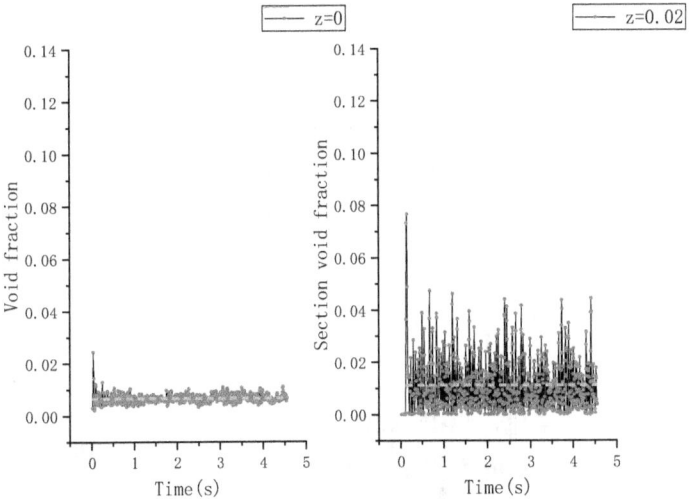

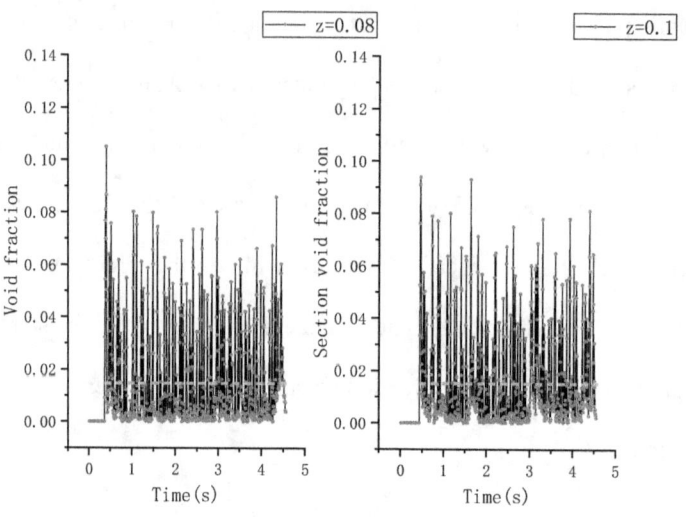

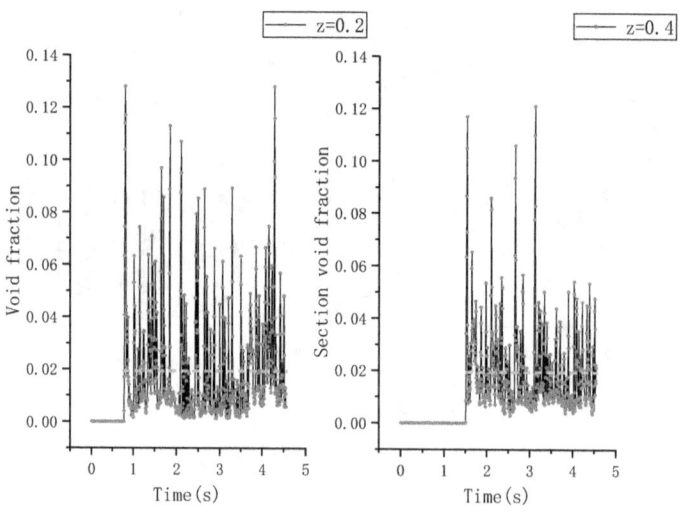

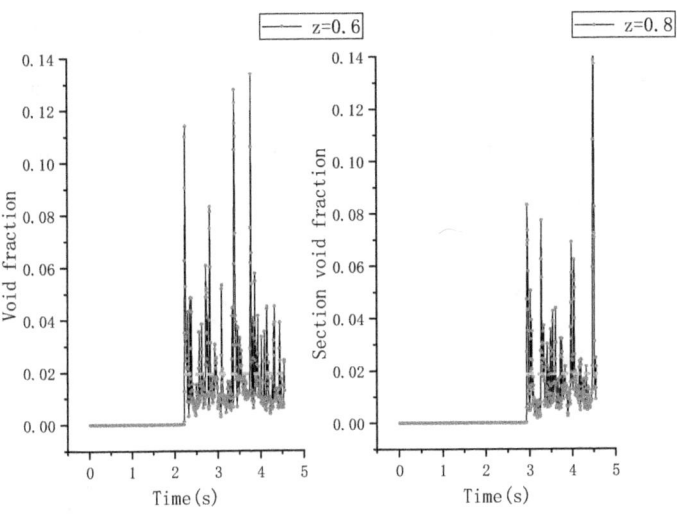

(a) The void fraction versus time and different planes

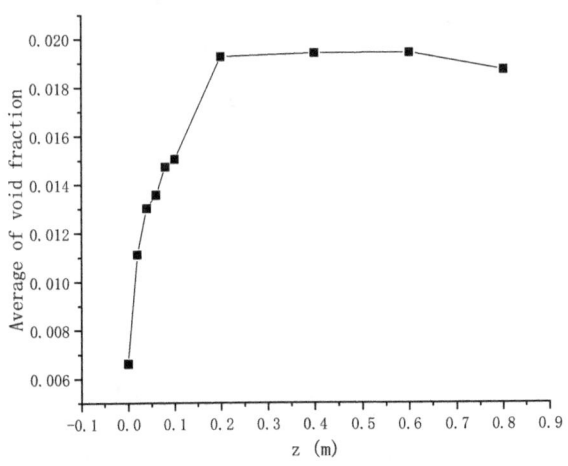

(b) The average of the void fraction

Fig. 19. Curve of void fraction, 0.5L/min helium flow rates

Fig. 20 shows the curve of void fraction versus time and 0.05L/min

helium flow rates. It can be found that the void fraction of each plane is generally very low under 0.05L/min helium flow rates. The maximum transient void fraction is only about 0.042, and the maximum average void fraction is even lower than 0.005. So, it is not rather meaningful to further analyze the void fraction.

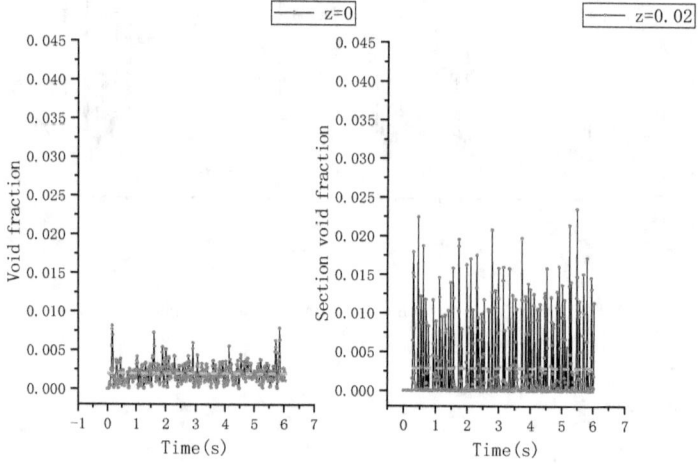

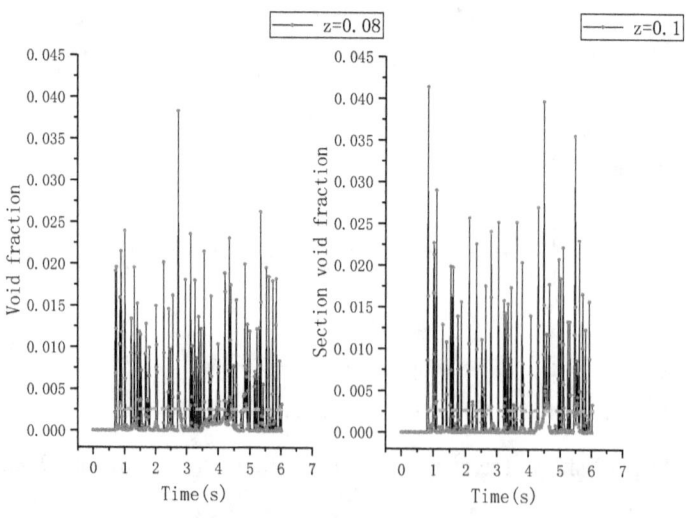

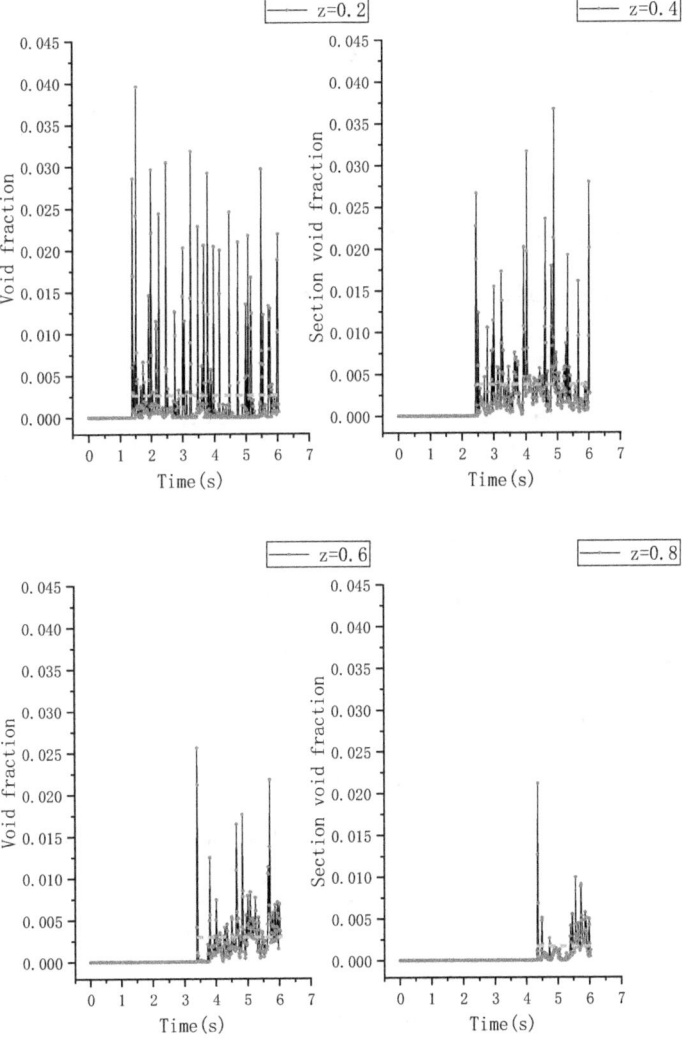

Fig. 20. Curve of void fraction, 0.05L/min helium flow rates

4. Summary and conclusion

In this study, taking the influence of bubbles on neutron detection as the background, a numerical simulation for the rising rules of helium bubbles in the cross-type flow channel has been carried out with CFD software. The major conclusions are as the following:

1. Because of flow disturbance caused by rising bubbles, the bubble coalescence exists widely in the middle area and bottom area of the flow channel (z<0.6m). The larger the helium flow rates are, the more frequent the coalescence will be. In the top area of the flow channel, due to the larger distance among the bubbles, the disturbance effect is small, so the coalescence is hard to happen. In the bottom area of the flow channel, the coalescence is most frequent, because of short distance;

2. During the process of bubble rising, the larger bubbles tend to move near to the tube wall, and some smaller bubbles tend to be far away from the tube wall (some can reach the one of the four corners of the cross-type channel), moving downward, due to the disturbance of the larger bubbles on the flow field;

3. When the helium flow rate is greater than 0.1L/min, the average value of the void fraction increases rapidly along the axial direction, and then tends to stabilize in the middle area and top area of the flow channel (z> 0.2m), and the greater the helium flow rate, the greater the void fraction.

References

[1] Vivek V. Buwa, D. Gerlach,F. Durst,E. Schlücker. Numerical simulations of bubble formation on submerged orifices: Period-1 and period-2 bubbling regimes[J]. *Chemical Engineering Science*, 2007,62(24): 7119-7132.

[2] D. Gerlach, N. Alleborn,V. Buwa,F. Durst. Numerical simulation of periodic bubble formation at a submerged orifice with constant gas flow rate[J]. *Chemical Engineering Science*,2006,62(7): 2109-2125.

[3] Yu Haijing. Numerical Simulation of Bubble Formation and Movement[D].Wuhan: Tianjin University,2010.

[4] Irfan Khan, Mingjun Wang, Yapei Zhang, Wenxi Tian, Guanghui Su, Suizheng Qiu, Two-Phase Bubbly Flow Simulation using CFD Method: A Review of Models for Interfacial Forces[J]. *Progress in Nuclear Energy*, 2020,125:1-17.

[5] Chong Chen, Mingjun Wang, Xiaohan Zhao, Haoran Ju, Xi Wang, Wenxi Tian, Suizheng Qiu, Guanghui Su. Numerical study on the single bubble rising behaviors under rolling conditions. *Nuclear Engineering and Design*, 2019, 349: 183-192.

[6] Li Guang. Two-Phase Flow Dynamical Simulations and Modelling of Bubble Column Reactors [D]. East China University of Science and Technology, 2010.

[7] Huang Ying. Numerical Study of Bubble Behavior in Vertical Rectangular Narrow Channel[D]. Harbin: Harbin Engineering University,2014.

[8] Wu Xuan, Jiao Jingjing. Expansion and detachment characteristics of bubble at downward nozzle of vertical flat pipe [J]. *CIESC Journal*,2016.67(5):1869-1877.

[9] Lu Wei. Experimental and Numerical Simulation Research on the Gas-Liquid Stirring Characteristics of Immersion Top-Blown from Single Orifice [D]. Wuhan: Wuhan University of Science and Technology,2016:11-19.

[10]Hideki Tsuge,Yusuke Tezuka,Masae Mitsudani. Bubble formation mechanism from downward nozzle—Effect of nozzle shape and operating parameters[J]. *Chemical Engineering Science*, 2005,61(10):3290-3298.

[11]Wu Xuan, Li Songyang. Numerical Simulation on Bubble Behavior at Nozzle of Vertical Flat Pipe [J]. Journal of Yangtze River Scientific Research Institute, 2019.36(1):68-73.

[12]Guangyuan Jin, Changqi Yan, Licheng Sun, Dianchuan Xing, Bao Zhou. Void fraction of dispersed bubbly flow in a narrow rectangular channel under rolling conditions[J]. *Progress in Nuclear Energy*, 2014, (70):256-265.

[13]Masaaki Hashida, Kosuke Hayashi, Akio Tomiyama. Rise velocities of single bubbles in a narrow channel between parallel flat plates[J]. *International Journal of Multiphase Flow*, 2019, (111): 285-293.

[14]Tang Jiapeng. Fluent 14.0 Super Learning Manual (in Chinese) [M]. Beijing: Post & Telecom Press, 2014: 30-38.

[15]ANSYS, Inc. (2016) ANSYS Fluent User's Guide, Release 17.2.

Publisher: Eliva Press SRL

Email: info@elivapress.com

A Book About My Pet

A Child's Creation

Randi Lynn Millward

Instructions:

This book is a children's activity book. The sentences are started but left incomplete for the child to finish in his or her own words. The adjacent pages are intentionally left blank for the child to illustrate with his or her own personal artwork.

The artist may color with crayons, tape photos onto the paper, or use any other age-appropriate parent-approved artistic medium that does not bleed through the paper.

ISBN 10: 1-943771-07-3
ISBN 13: **978-1-943771-07-3**

More books by this author may be found online at
www.Amazon.com and other participating retailers.

A Book About My Pet

By

Age: _____

Date: _____

_____

_____

_____

_____

My pet is a

My pet is named

_____

_____

_____

_____ .

I like when my pet

_____

_____

_____

_____ .

My pet likes
when I

_____

_____

_____

_____ .

II

My pet
doesn't like

_____

_____

_____

_____

My pet
is really
good at

_____

_____

_____

_____

My pet feels

_____

_____

_____

_____ .

I smile when my pet

_____

_____

_____

_____ .

I have fun when my pet and I

_____

_____

_____

_____ .

My pet
looks sleepy
when

_____

_____

_____

_____.

My favorite
thing to do
with my pet
is

_____

_____

_____

_____.

My favorite
thing about
my pet is

_____

_____

_____

_____

_____.

_____

_____

_____

I wish my pet
could

My pet likes to eat

_____

_____

_____

_____ .

When I'm
not home,
my pet

_____

_____

_____

_____.

When I come home,
my pet

_____

_____

_____

_____ .

_____

_____

_____

_____

I love my pet
because

The End